The Little Pocket Book of
Pug Wisdom

REMEMBER TO STOP AND SMELL THE ROSES.
IF NECESSARY, YOU SHOULD ALSO PEE ON THEM.

The Little Pocket Book of
Pug Wisdom
Lessons in life and love for the well-rounded pug

Gemma Correll

DOG 'n' BONE

This combined edition published in 2016 by Dog 'n' Bone Books
an imprint of Ryland Peters & Small Ltd

20–21 Jockey's Fields
London WC1R 4BW

341 E 116th St
New York, NY 10029

Previously published in 2013 by Dog 'n' Bone Books under the titles
A Pug's Guide to Etiquette and *A Pug's Guide to Dating*

www.rylandpeters.com

10 9 8 7 6 5 4 3 2 1

Text copyright © Gemma Correll 2016
Design and illustration copyright © Dog 'n' Bone Books 2016

A CIP catalog record for this book is available from the Library of Congress
and the British Library.

ISBN-13: 978 1 909313 86 6

Printed in China

Editor: Pete Jorgensen
Designer: Jerry Goldie
Illustrator: Gemma Correll

CONTENTS

MANNERS & ETIQUETTE

THE WELL-ROUNDED PUG

An ancient breed descended from the Chinese *Lo-Chiang-Sze* dog, the pug is a proud, handsome, and fragrant creature. He is the loveable champion of the canine world. A snorting, wheezing, farting ambassador for small dogs; not much bigger than a cat, yet exhibiting the sturdy rotundness of an unusually excitable warthog. Bred many centuries ago by the monks of Tibet, beloved pet of royals and aristocrats including Queen Victoria and Marie Antoinette, and muse to artists such as William Hogarth, the modern pug must strive to honor his legacy as a special, superior creature.

Custom emphatically dictates that a well-bred pug should abide by the strict rules of etiquette and decorum.

Navigating this potential minefield of manners may initially prove difficult for a young pug not yet experienced in the conventions of polite society, but he will quickly discover the satisfaction that following the rules can bring. He must realize that actions such as begging for food, molting all over the sofa, and relieving himself on the grumpy neighbor's front lawn are essential facets of pug protocol. It is simply not proper to behave like a common dog—the pug is a different breed altogether. He should understand the matters of socializing, courting, and licking, and, above all, seek to conduct himself in a winsome and unwaveringly squishy fashion.

A pleasant manner comes naturally to the pug, born as he is to the possession of good looks, a pleasant temperament, and an excellent knowledge of where the food is to be found. The pug's duty is to amuse and entertain his human; to greet him or her with enthusiasm on their return from an outing, however fleeting (even a short bathroom visit is worthy of at least ten minutes of frantic jumping and yelping); and to make himself useful in a variety of ways. He must strive to maintain a facade of utter melancholy, masking an inner world positively brimming with love, joy, and undigested kibble. The well—bred pug understands that he must undulate between manic tomfoolery and near—catatonic sleepiness, endeavoring to maintain a steady 20 hours of sleep per day. He will do well to heed the pug's motto, *Carpe Kibble* (or "Seize the Kibble") and remember that foremost covenant of Pugdom: You may lead a pug to water, but you cannot make him have a bath.

PERSONAL APPEARANCE & GROOMING

THE GOLDEN RULE

Lick. Lick often; lick thoroughly. Lick until you can lick no more. Lick the air if necessary.

ANATOMY OF THE GENTEEL PUG

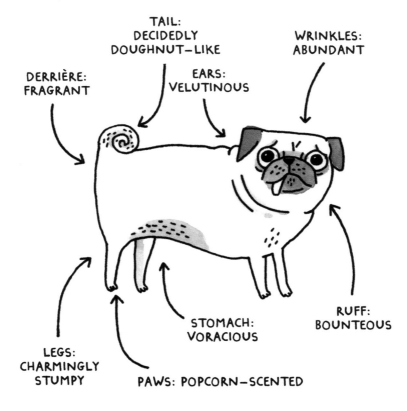

TAIL:
DECIDEDLY
DOUGHNUT–LIKE

WRINKLES:
ABUNDANT

DERRIÈRE:
FRAGRANT

EARS:
VELUTINOUS

LEGS:
CHARMINGLY
STUMPY

PAWS: POPCORN–SCENTED

STOMACH:
VORACIOUS

RUFF:
BOUNTEOUS

REGARDING PUG HAIR

A well—bred pug is altruistic and magnanimous with his favors, bestowing generous gifts of hair unto his home and unto his human.

GROOMING

Grooming is of the utmost importance and can be quite pleasurable.

NAIL CLIPPING

A nail clipping session should never be submitted to without a vehement and obstreperous display of one's vexation.

COMPLETING ONE'S TOILETTE

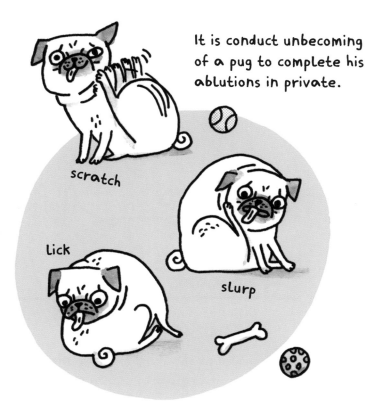

It is conduct unbecoming of a pug to complete his ablutions in private.

scratch

lick

slurp

ON SUNBATHING

A pale belly is positively vulgar. Any opportunity
to sunbathe should be immediately seized upon.

CLOTHING: DRESSING IN STUPID OUTFITS

It is an unfortunate fact of life that many humans are wont to dress innocent pugs in ridiculous outfits. When submitting to these indignities, it is important to maintain a stiff upper lip and air of nonchalance at all times.

Selecting a Nom de Plume

Cultivate a mysterious and alluring personality by adopting many pseudonyms.

BATH TIME

A genteel pug is never guilty of the sin of allowing his human to bathe unchaperoned.

Regarding the Cone

A well-bred pug maintains his dignity, even at times of utmost discomfiture.

THE ART OF CONVERSATION

It is of great importance, in the formation of good manners, that a young pug should be accustomed to mingle in polite society.

PUGS AT HOME

THE MORNING ROUTINE:
WAKING UP

Upon rising, preferably at a suitably early hour, you should ensure that you tread most thoroughly upon the face, bosom, and genitals of your sleeping owner.

THE PAW IN THE FACE

THE EAR LICK

THE PARP

THE SUFFOCATION

The Morning Routine: Closed Doors

In the home, a blocked entryway or thoroughfare must never be tolerated. Should one be encountered, it is advisable to scratch at the obstruction and whine pathetically.
Once the door is opened for you, however, do not feel obliged to use it.

The Morning Routine: Leaving the House

IF I SIT ON YOUR FOOT,
YOU WON'T BE ABLE
TO GO ANYWHERE.

MEALTIMES: TAKING CHARGE

It is imperative that you preside over all activity that takes place in the kitchen. The ideal position for satisfactory supervision is directly beneath the cook's feet.

MEALTIMES: THE KIBBLE

To maintain a healthy digestive system, from time to time eat at speed so that you may then immediately puke the contents of your stomach upon the expensive Persian carpet.

GURGLE

BURP

Mealtimes: Timetable

A strict mealtime regime and timetable must be adhered to. Breakfast and dinner should be served no later than one minute after the specified time. In the event of a delay, you are permitted to theatrically voice your grievances.

Useful Services

A well—bred pug endeavors to make himself indispensable to his human by providing a variety of useful services.

SPA TREATMENTS

LICK

MASSAGE

BOOK REST

PILLOW WARMING

ENTERTAINING

OW OWW OWWW

SNORING

SNORE

PARP

SNORE

SNORE

SNORE

SNORE

SNORE

It is a pug's prerogative to snore,
to snore loudly, and to snore continuously.

In the Bedroom

A well-bred pug will always play the buffoon, even when sleeping. He should twitch extravagantly and make unusual noises, preferably while drooling profusely.

PUG POSITIONS

THE GRUMP

THE LOAF

THE BELLY RUB?

THE SLUMP

THE YAWN 'N' STRETCH

THE CHIN REST

THE SYMPATHY VOTE

THE PAW TUCK

THE SPRAWL

THE FROG

THE DOWNWARD FACING PUG

THE TWIST 'N' SNIFF

THE SLUMP O'GUILT

THE HEAD TILT

THE KITTY

THE PENSIVE PAW LICK

THE SIT-UP

THE NEW FRONTIER

THE CROSSOVER STRETCH

THE SIDE SLUMP

THE THINKER

THE HANG-OUT

ENTERTAINING

APERITIFS

Tissues, procured from your guests' pockets and handbags, make delightful appetizers.

TABLE MANNERS

A respectable pug will ensure that for the duration of a meal he is seated immediately below the human guest considered most likely to drop tidbits.

CLEANING

It is looked upon as the height of vulgarity to allow any leftover food to remain on the crockery.

WATERING HOLE

The usual social graces are considered unnecessary at the watering hole, where it is advisable to push your way in and make as much mess as possible.

ENTERTAINING GUESTS

During any respectable dinner party, your guests will appreciate a well-formed poo, or noisy bum-licking display, in the middle of the dining room.

On Farting

It is considered polite to fart heavily after your host has served you a meal.

BATHROOM BREAKS

Follow all guests to the bathroom. Do not wait for an invitation—they will welcome your presence.

After Dinner Entertainment

Upon finishing dinner, you may wish to instigate a rousing game of "Repeatedly Pushing One's Ball Under the Chair" or "Stealing Things from the Laundry Basket."

TOY DISPLAY

When entertaining guests, a pug of good breeding will always demonstrate a display of his toys.

PARLOR TRICKS

Humans, in their infinite feeble-mindedness, will be impressed by even the smallest repertoire of tricks. Do not give up your skills too freely—encourage them to bribe you with treats and belly rubs.

"SIT" "PAW" "HIGH FIVE"

"UP" "SPIN" "SPEAK"

SPORTS & RECREATION

THE PILE UP

On your introduction to society, it is highly recommended that you acquaint yourself with your fellow pugs by taking part in a traditional "Pile Up."

TOY TEST

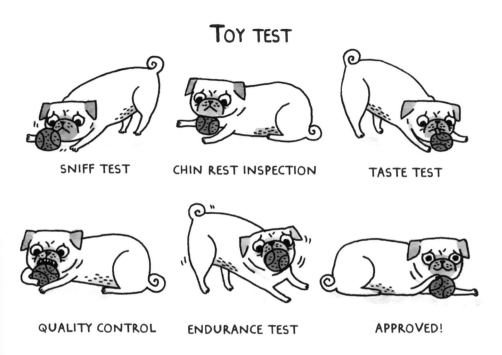

SNIFF TEST

CHIN REST INSPECTION

TASTE TEST

QUALITY CONTROL

ENDURANCE TEST

APPROVED!

When offered a new toy, do not immediately pounce upon it—this is considered the very height of bad manners. Instead, perform a series of rigorous tests in order to ascertain the toy's worthiness of being added to your repertoire.

Playtime

A well-bred pug will find amusement partaking in the following activities...

suckle

TOY SUCKLING

scoot scoot

BUM SCOOTING

wriggle wriggle

CATCHING AND EATING LIVE SPIDERS

THE CUSHION BULLDOZING GAME

FETCH

Never play "Fetch"—this evinces lack of proper manners and is better left to creatures of a lower social standing, such as Labradors and humans.

OVEREXERTION

Strenuous exercise should
be kept to a minimum,
with the obvious exception
of the thrice daily
doctrinal "Pug Run."

MAKING CALLS

When paying a social call, a pug should make himself entirely familiar with every corner of the host's abode.

BIDDING FAREWELL

SHE IS GOING TO LOVE
THAT HALF-CHEWED PIG'S EAR
I LEFT ON HER PILLOW.

Having paid his adieux, a polite pug will always endeavor
to leave a small parting gift for the host, who will doubtless
be delighted to chance upon it (preferably whilst barefoot)
some minutes later.

ETIQUETTE OF THE STREET

BARKING

It is considered highly appropriate to bark whenever you feel that it is necessary and at absolutely any time of the day or, indeed, the night.

On occasion, a pug should bark for no discernable reason at all.

YOU MAY BARK AT:

TRASH BAGS

INANIMATE OBJECTS

BIG, SCARY-LOOKING DOGS

SMALL CHILDREN

THE VACUUM CLEANER

YOUR SHADOW

In Regard to Inclement Weather

A pug of good breeding does not trouble himself
to leave the house when it is raining.

PUDDLE AVOIDANCE

Nor does he acquiesce to traverse a puddle.

THE DAILY CONSTITUTIONAL

The search for the perfect spot for your morning evacuation should be at your leisure and should always exceed ten minutes in length. Especially if it is snowing.

POOP DANCE

Upon the completion of your aforementioned duties, it is customary to perform a dance.

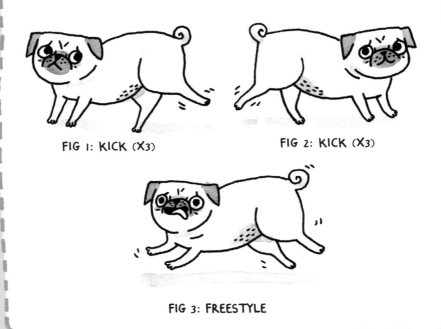

FIG 1: KICK (X3)

FIG 2: KICK (X3)

FIG 3: FREESTYLE

STREET SALUTATIONS

You should recognize acquaintances with a courteous bum sniff and face lick.

Strangers may be greeted with either frenzied, cacophonous barking or gratuitous snogging. Use your discretion.

Encountering the Ignoramuses

A pug may find himself accosted by poorly educated peasants who make impolite insinuations regarding his breeding and apparent similarity to "That dog off *Men in Black*." Take pity on these poor inerudite souls, for they do not know any better.

DROP & ROLL

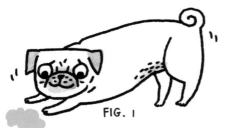

FIG. 1

FIG. 2

FIG. 3

Upon encountering something which appears to be dead or rotting, the recommended action is the "Stop, Drop, and Roll" routine, as detailed above.

SNIFFING

One of the foremost pleasures in a young pug's life is the delicious sniffing of morning air, which should be inhaled deeply and appreciated like a fine bowl of puddle water.

A Final Word

Above all, remember that, as a pug, you were born a fundamentally superior creature and are therefore the true master of any respectable household.

And don't let them forget it.

SECTION 2
RELATIONSHIPS

PUG LOVE

Wrinkly of face and fragrant of backside, the pug is one of nature's most romantic creations. A twenty-pound, wheezing, farting Lothario with an undeniably magnetic allure that no creature—of the canine persuasion or otherwise—can resist.

Nonetheless, even for these naturally amorous and handsome creatures, the world of love can be a daunting and confusing place; a minefield of potential mistakes and misjudgments. The pug who abides, as most do, by the laws of etiquette and decorum that govern his kind, will understand the need to tread carefully, to study and strive to comprehend the conventions that govern the world of curly-tailed courting.

To the casual observer, it may appear that the pug, possessed as he is with natural charm and charisma, dashing good looks, and an infinite repertoire of alluring snorty noises, finds it easy to attract any number of admirers. And indeed, this is fundamentally the case—most creatures of any intelligence, upon meeting him, are immediately smitten.

However, even the most confident pug may require guidance in the sometimes bewildering world of modern dating. For example, he must learn how to present himself in a personal ad or at a speed-dating event, or he must determine how to find the most suitable and romantic location for a first date.

Essentially, he must become a dedicated scholar in the art of love, pondering upon the very fundamentals of flirtation, seeking to master the basic principles of poetry, song, and dance, and conquering the elementary techniques of kissing and snuggling.

Once comfortably ensconced in a relationship, the pug must endeavor to keep the "flame" of love alive, ensuring that the erstwhile heady days of puppy love, although in the past, are never forgotten. He must never forget a special occasion such as an anniversary or canceled veterinary appointment, ensuring that he lavishes gifts and passionate, intense kisses upon his sweetheart at every opportunity.

Sadly, the pug's unconditionally loving and devoted temperament can work against him in the event of a break-up. He, sensitive creature that he is, may find himself quite undone by the painful heartbreak that so often accompanies a separation. One hesitates to label the pug with the hyperbolic terms "neurotic" or "obsessive" but he does seem to take all forms of separation, whether from his human, his sweetheart, or even from a favorite toy, particularly badly. It is imperative, therefore, that he learns to cope with rejection and heartache in a useful and healthy manner.

The love of a pug is faithful and unwavering. He is a devoted partner; a generous and caring paramour with a face full of wrinkles and a heart of gold. As the old saying goes...

"To know a pug is to love him."

BREAKING THE ICE

FIRST IMPRESSIONS

First impressions count. Take care to maintain a memorably fragrant derrière at all times. After all, you never know who you might be lucky enough to bump into!

Pick-up Lines

Come here often?

You must be tired...
You've been running through
my mind all day.

Did you just roll in fox poop or is
that your natural aroma?

Hey baby, I like your wrinkles.

SPEED DATING

Attending a speed dating event is a great, fun way to meet other lonely hearts.

CHANCE ENCOUNTERS

Romance might not be the first thing on your mind when visiting the vet (it's more likely to be a desperate urge to pee on the examination table) but love can blossom in the most unexpected places...

How To Tell if She Likes You

A pug shows affection quite readily, so it can be difficult to differentiate between a naturally friendly demeanor and real affection.

Watch out for these signs that she wants to be more than "just friends"...

She mirrors your body language...

I AVERAGE 250 LICKS PER MINUTE.

She shows off in front of you...

She tries the old "Damsel in Distress" act...

HELP!

She brings you gifts...

Asking Her Out

Choose your moment and your location wisely. Pick a time and a place where she is relaxed and comfortable, like just after a good poop in the grumpy next–door neighbor's front garden.

REMAIN POSITIVE

Don't be intimidated! Remember, you may be small but you are perfectly formed.

Your potential partner will almost certainly say "yes." Who can resist a face like that?

REJECTION

Don't be disheartened if she says "no"—it's her loss.

SIGH

However, you should ham it up as much as possible in order to secure more sympathetic belly rubs, and possibly extra kibble, from your human.

Sigh repeatedly, squeeze yourself into tight spaces, and generally mope around looking pathetic. Humans are weak. They will fall for it.

Personal Ads

CAT (f) with sociopathic tendencies seeks tom cat for chair scratching and tail chasing during the day. Must be spayed and have own flea collar.

FAWN,
NEUTERED PUG (3)
With double-curled tail seeks easy-going lady for ear licking and maybe more. Must enjoy bacon, barking at inanimate objects, and cuddles on the sofa. GSOH, NS, SWM, PUG
Box No. 652732

EXOTIC PARROT with authority issues, GSOH seeks similar. Must enjoy incessant chatter and own own cage. NS, NSFW, BOX No. 344277

WHIPPET, F, 21 (in dog years) looking for true love. All breeds considered. Athletic build, short attention span. Must like running and chasing cats.

If you are having trouble finding a suitable partner using the conventional route, you might like to try online dating, or you could place a personal ad in the newspaper.

DATING

FINDING MR. OR MRS. RIGHT

Love knows no size, color, or breed.

Although the object of your affection may not always share this philosophy.

FIRST DATE

Hurrah! Your crush has agreed to a rendezvous.
But where to go? Here are some ideas:

A romantic stroll presents the perfect
opportunity for you to impress your
sweetheart with your worldly knowledge...

I JUST LOVE PASTRIES.

While a visit to a local café allows you to get to know each other in a comfortable environment, with the added bonus of a floor full of crumbs on which to nibble.

If you are culture vultures, you may both enjoy a visit to a gallery or for hip young urbanites a street art exhibition.

There are those who say that you should never sleep together on the first date. But we say—do whatever makes you happy!

GROOMING

Of course, you'll want to look—and smell—your very best for your first date.

Exclusively for pugs

With hints of badger

Earthy and bright

A classic

What to Wear

A harness and leash are perfectly appropriate first-date attire, but if you really want to make an impression, ask your human to choose an outfit for you.

Something understated and subtle, yet undeniably sexy—like a lobster costume or a giant banana suit—should do the trick.

Romantic Keepsakes

When you visit your sweetheart at home, be sure to leave a memento for her to remember you by. Perhaps a generous sprinkling of fur atop a contrasting-colored sofa...

A selection of decorative paw prints across a freshly mopped floor...

Or simply your own delightfully pungent natural scent.

BEAUTIFUL!

LOOKING YOUR BEST

An enlightened pug knows how to make the best of whatever he has to work with.

ROMANCE

POETRY

> OH, BLACK IS THE COLOR
> OF MY TRUE LOVE'S COAT,
> HER FACE SO FLAT AND HER WRINKLY THROAT.
> THE BIGGEST EYES AND THE SCRATCHIEST PAWS
> I LOVE THE GROUND ON
> WHICH SHE SNORES.

Nothing is more romantic than poetry. Except maybe a box of heart-shaped meaty treats (hint hint).

ROSED ARE RED,
VIOLETS ARE BLUE.
IF I SNIFF YOUR BUM,
WILL YOU SNIFF
MY BUM TOO?

MY LOVE FOR YOU IS LIKE MY MORNING PEE;
IT GOES ON AND ON AND ON... AND ON.

MY LOVE FOR YOU IS LIKE A SNEEZE;
SLOPPY, WET, AND IN YOUR FACE.

MY LOVE FOR YOU IS LIKE A SQUEAKY TOY;
IT DRIVES ME CRAZY.

MY LOVE FOR YOU IS LIKE A BOWL
FULL OF KIBBLE;
DELICIOUS AND... MMMM...
WAIT, WHAT WAS I TALKING ABOUT?

DANCE

The art of dance is sensual and passionate. Here are a few moves that you might like to try...

THE DANCE OF THE FLYING PILLOWS

LE GRAND JETÉ
(AUX DEUX
HUNGRY PUGS)

THE POOPY
KICKIN' JIVE

THE BOOTY
WIGGLE

THE CARPET SURF
BOOGIE

THE FART 'N' TWIST

THE
DINNERTIME
JITTERBUG

THE TAIL CHASIN' REEL

KISSING

It's no secret that we pugs love to kiss. The most popular smooching style is of course the traditional, vigorous, and incessant "pug lick," which is used to show affection toward another creature, whether animal, human (familiar or strange), or inanimate object.

Here are some other kissing styles that are favored among pug—kind...

ESKIMO KISS

FRENCH KISS

EAR NIBBLES

NECKING

THREE—WAY KISS

STARGAZING

The night sky is the
window to the universe.
Spend a romantic evening
stargazing with your beloved.
Look out for famous constellations
like CANIS MINOR (the little dog)
and CATTUS STUPIDUS (the stupid cat).

SERENADING

Pugs are known to possess beautiful singing voices. Make the most of this natural talent by performing a heartfelt, sentimental composition extolling the many virtues of your inamorata—a cappella, of course.

SPECIAL OCCASIONS

VALENTINE'S DAY

On Valentine's Day, it is traditional for sweethearts to exchange gifts.

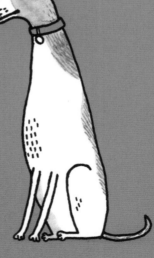

Here are a few great gift ideas:

SEXY LINGERIE
(WORN)*

TREAT SELECTION
BOX

BEEF
TURKEY
LAMB
FISH

TEDDY BEAR*

I LOVE YOU

BOUQUET OF
USED TISSUES

*FOR CHEWING PURPOSES

A Romantic Weekend

Spend some quality time together. Why not treat yourself and your partner to some fancy spa treatments, expertly administered by your personal human–assistant?

AYURVEDIC
BELLY MASSAGE

WET DISHTOWEL
BODY WRAP
(SUMMER SPECIAL)

DETOXING
FULL-BODY
BRUSH

KIBBLE AND WET FOOD FACIAL

(may be accompanied
by a push-the-bowl-
around-the-floor
workout)

We recommend
that you avoid the pedicure.

A Romantic Dinner

Celebrate special occasions, like anniversaries or canceled veterinary appointments, with a romantic dinner in a suitably enchanting location.

Try the kitchen floor or the back yard for a delightful al fresco tête-à-tête.

Menu Suggestions

APPETIZERS

Medallions of cat poop nestled on a bed of crispy ryegrass.

Assortment of amuse—bouches.

ENTRÉES

Artisan underwear atop a purée of pinecones.

Pan—fried tissues in an organic peanut butter jus.

DESSERTS

Hamster droppings in a decadent vomit compote.

TO DRINK...

"Yellow Snow" margarita.

Our special "Puddle Water" martini.

Gourmet "Day—Old" coffee.

Toilet water sorbet served in a French—style tennis ball.

Anniversaries

It is a custom among pugs and other dogs to celebrate anniversaries with gifts that symbolize the number of (dog) years that they have been together.

1 YEAR

TURKEY & RICE

7 YEARS

KIBBLE

14 YEARS

BISCUITS

21 YEARS

PEANUT BUTTER

28 YEARS

BONE

35 YEARS

BACON

Also commonly performed during anniversary celebrations is the ancient pug tradition of "THE LICKING OF THE FLOOR."

This ritual should always be undertaken with purpose and dedication. A floor–licking ceremony can last anywhere between a couple of minutes to several hours.

It may be performed on any surface, including carpet, linoleum, and concrete.

Another popular anniversary custom is the "Dinnertime Observance," whereupon the happy pug couple maintain a thrice–daily vigil underneath the hallowed "table of the humans," waiting in anticipation for sacred "tidbits" to fall.

This ritual has deep significance. The table symbolizes life, the humans represent fate, and the crumbs are symbolic of everlasting love.

Fighting over the crumbs is generally thought to be inauspicious.

Pet Names

Once a couple have celebrated their first anniversary together, they will no doubt have developed pet names for each other. These monikers are terms of endearment used by a romantically involved couple, often inspired by a physical characteristic or personality trait.

LICKLICK

SNORTFACE MCDRIBBLE

FATBOY

MR WRINKLES

LITTLE PIRATE

GRUMPS

TOOTHY O'WORMFACE

SIR STINKSALOT

WONKY

MATTERS OF THE HEART

LOVE IS...

Patience and understanding...

LOVE IS...

all about...

two people...

PREPARED TO
COMPROMISE...

LOVE IS...

Feeling comfortable and relaxed together...

And accepting each other, flaws and all.

Love is
unconditional.

KEEPING THE ROMANCE ALIVE

The couple that...

CHIN RESTS TOGETHER

HEAD TILTS TOGETHER

SUNBATHES TOGETHER

... stays together.

SHOWING YOU CARE

Make sure you let your loved one know how
much they mean to you.

Say "I love you" every day in your own special way.
(A lingering wet lick will almost certainly also
be appreciated.)

JE T'AIME
(FRENCH)

IK HOU VAN JOU
(DUTCH)

TE AMO
(SPANISH)

JAG ÄLSKAR DIG
(SWEDISH)

SNORT SNORT
(PUG)

DON'T GET STUCK IN A RUT

When you first get together, it's all very exciting and new. After a while, though, you may find yourself in such a familiar routine that you end up taking each other for granted. Avoid this by keeping things exciting.

Try some new positions in bed, such as...

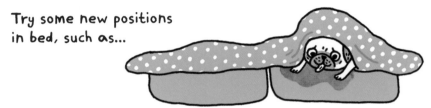

THE PILLOW LICKER

THE PILLOW FARTER

Your human will appreciate these too.

AFFAIRS

Pugs are generally faithful
creatures, but a young,
naive pug may be tempted
to snuggle with someone
besides his significant
other.

It's not the end of the world, unless you
are tempted to snuggle the hamster...

Then it might be (for him anyway).

BREAKUPS

NIGGLES

In a long—term relationship, you may find that some things begin to annoy you about your partner.

WHY CAN'T SHE GIVE ME SOME
SPACE FOR ONCE?

WHY DOES HE ALWAYS STEAL
MY FAVORITE TOYS?

WHY DOES HE
HAVE TO SNORE
SO LOUDLY?

Every relationship has
its ups and downs.

THE END IS NIGH

Sadly, some relationships must come to an end, and a breakup can be utterly devastating for the sensitive pug.

SYMPTOMS OF HEARTBREAK

You might find that you have problems eating.

Your sleeping patterns may become irregular.

You may even suffer from physical symptoms such as gastrointestinal upsets.

GETTING OVER IT

A breakup is tough, but you can get through it. You are a pug! Master of the universe! King of the curly tails! You can do anything! You can lick your own nose, for goodness sake.

Remember to stay active.
(Never neglect your thrice daily "Pug Run.")

Take time out to reflect.

Don't forget to look after yourself.

LETTING IT OUT

Try some stress-relieving exercises, such as barking at the TV. (This is particularly effective when performed during your human's favorite TV shows.)

SOCIALIZING

Spending some quality time with your best friends will
soon help you forget about things.

JE NE REGRETTE RIEN

Even if a love affair ends badly (you were a pug, she was a Labradoodle... the rest is history...), don't look back with sadness or regrets.

Leave the past behind you, like a particularly stinky fart, and move on.

The future awaits! And it's bacon flavored.

HOPE

Never forget, there are plenty more dogs in the park and someone special out there for every pug.

A Final Word

A wise pug once said...

All you need is love,
kibble, and a de-worming tablet
every three to six months.

ACKNOWLEDGMENTS

Thank you Anthony, my partner in life, studio, and stupid in-jokes (Baka-ahh).

Thanks Team Little Red Roaster and Lucy (I'm still cross with you, though) and to all my friends and family for putting up with, nay, actively encouraging my ridiculous pug obsession.

Thank you to everyone at Dog 'n' Bone and Cico, especially Pete Jorgensen and, of course, one big belly rubbing thank you to my muses
Mr. Pickles and Bella for never ceasing to amuse and inspire me.